GYMNASTICS
PARALLEL BARS AND HORIZONTAL BAR

JOANNE MATTERN

The Rourke Corporation, Inc.
Vero Beach, Florida 32964

PROJECT EDITOR:
Genger Thorn is a professional member of USA and AAU gymnastics associations. She is USA safety certified and an associate member of the US Elite Coaches Association (USECA). Genger is currently a girls team coach and director at East Coast Gymnastics, Merritt Island, Florida.

PHOTO CREDITS:
All photo Tony Gray except page 4 © Reuters/Mike Blake/Archive Photos

EDITORIAL SERVICES:
Janice L. Smith for Penworthy Learning Systems

Library of Congress Cataloging-in-Publication Data

Mattern, Joanne, 1963-
    Gymnastics / by Joanne Mattern
        p. cm.
    Includes bibliographical references and indexes.
    Contents: [1] Training and fitness — [2] The pommel horse and the rings — [3] The vault — [4] Balance beam and floor exercises — [5] Uneven parallel bars — [6] Parallel bars and horizontal bar.
    ISBN 0-86593-571-8 (v.1). — ISBN 0-86593-568-8 (v. 2). — ISBN 0-86593-566-1 (v. 3). — ISBN 0-86593-567.X (v. 4). — ISBN 0-86593-569-6 (v. 5). — ISBN 0-86593-570-X (v. 6)
    1. Gymnastics for children Juvenile literature. [1. Gymnastics.] I. Title
GV464.5.M38 1999
796.44—dc21   99-27924
                                                                          CIP

Printed in the USA

TABLE OF CONTENTS

The parallel bars always have been one of the favorites in gymnastics competition.

THE EQUIPMENT

The parallel bars and the horizontal bar are both events for men. Succeeding in these events requires a good sense of timing, excellent balance, strong arms and shoulders, and a flexible body.

The parallel bars were invented in the early 1800s by Friedrich Jahn of Germany. Jahn is known as the father of modern gymnastics because he developed several events. Jahn was also responsible for making gymnastics a part of the European educational system.

When Jahn first invented the bars, he thought his students would use them to practice for **pommel horse** (PAHM ul HAWRS) events. However, the bars were so popular that they soon became a separate event.

When the parallel bars were first used, gymnasts performed very slowly. They used the strength of their arms and shoulders to hold difficult positions. Today, parallel bars are used very differently. A **routine** (roo TEEN) on the bars includes lots of swings, somersaults, and other movements that send the gymnast soaring above and below the bars. Gymnasts also receive extra credit for performing moves on just one bar. A routine also must include at least one move performed below the bars.

The Parallel Bars

The bars **apparatus** (AP uh RAT uhs) consists of two wooden bars supported by metal uprights and placed side by side on the floor. The bars can be set at no more than 67 inches (1.7 m) during competition, but lower heights are used in practice. The bars are placed 19 to 25 inches (48 to 63-1/2 cm) apart for competitions.

★ COACH'S CORNER

A Woman's Event?

Both men and women competed on the parallel bars until the 1950s. Then the uneven parallel bars were developed by changing the height and position of one of the bars. The uneven bars became a women's event because it allowed female gymnasts to perform stunts more suited to their smaller, lighter bodies.

SIDE VIEW OF PARALLEL BARS

138 inches (3.5 m)

67 inches (1.7 m)

END VIEW OF PARALLEL BARS

19-25 inches (48-63.5 cm)

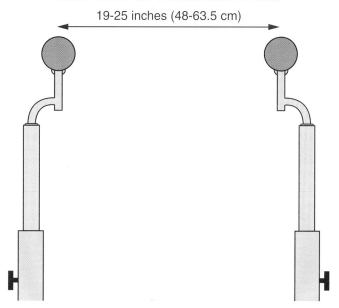

The dimensions of the parallel bars

The Horizontal Bar

The horizontal bar is also known as the high bar. The bar is made of steel and is very flexible. A horizontal bar can bend up to four inches (about 10 cm) as the gymnast moves on it! This flexibility helps the gymnast gain momentum as he swings around the bar.

The horizontal bar is supported by metal uprights at either end. These uprights can stand on a base or be inserted directly into the floor. Steel cables keep the uprights steady. The bar itself is about 94 inches (slightly less the 2.5 m) long and stands 100 inches (just over 2.5 m) above the floor.

The horizontal bar is considered the most spectacular men's event. The gymnast can be as high as 14 feet (more than 4 m) off the ground, moves very quickly and is often upside-down!

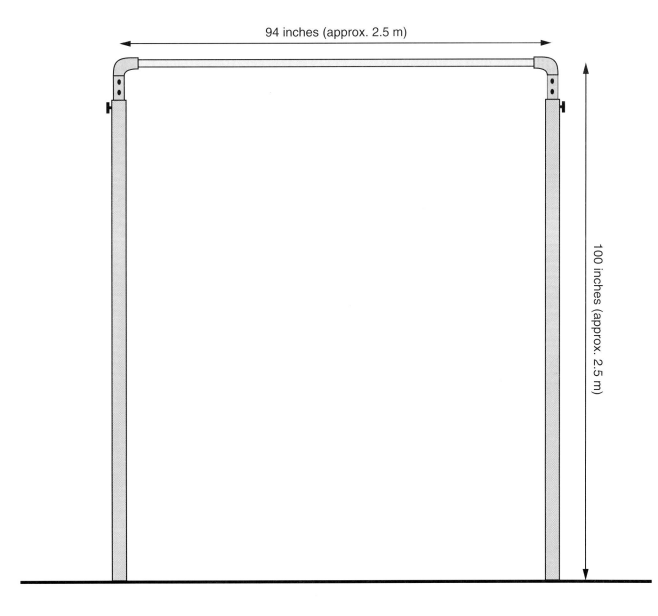

94 inches (approx. 2.5 m)

100 inches (approx. 2.5 m)

The dimensions of the horizontal bar

The simplest way to mount the horizontal bar is to walk up to the bar and jump—or have a coach lift you.

MOUNTING THE BARS

The Horizontal Bar

Getting onto an apparatus is called a **mount** (MOUNT). There are no specific mounts for the horizontal bar. Instead, simply approach the bar and jump straight up. Grip the bar with your hands shoulder-width apart and let your body hang straight down. Avoid arching, or curving your back.

As soon as you are on the bar, pump your legs slightly to start a swing. This swing will give you the momentum to prepare for your first movement.

While swinging to get your momentum, you should arch under the bar then kick hard to a **hollow** (HAHL O) extended position. While swinging backward again, **arch** (AHRCH) under the bar and rise in a hollow position with your feet trailing your body.

Make sure you have a firm grip before starting your routine.

The Parallel Bars

There are several ways to mount the parallel bars. You will want to start with some very basic mounts.

Straight-Arm Support Mount

1. Stand at one end of the bars with your back straight and your feet together. You should be close enough to grasp the bars in an **overgrip** (O ver GRIP). This means that your fingers should be curled over the top of the bar and your thumbs underneath. Your elbows should be bent comfortably.
2. Bend your knees and jump straight up. At the same time, push down on your hands and then straighten your arms.
3. End with your head high and your back and legs straight. Your full weight should be supported on your arms.

★ DID YOU KNOW?

Variations on the
Single-Leg Cut-On Mount

You can change the single-leg cut-on mount (see page 15) by swinging your right leg out instead of your left. Later, you can try a double-leg cut-off. In this move, both legs shift to one side and travel outside the bars. Lift one hand to allow both legs to travel through the open space together, then drop them between the bars.

To perform the single-leg cut-on mount start in the straight-arm
support position.

Single-Leg Cut-On Mount

1. Start with a straight-arm support mount.

2. As you straighten your legs and move above the bars, hold your right leg so that it passes between the bars. Lift your left leg out to the side so that it passes outside the left bar.

3. Next, swing your left leg over the top of the bar and drop it to the inside. Lift your left hand from the bar at the same time to let your leg pass through the open space.

4. As soon as your leg passes through the space, grab the bar again. End in the straight-arm support position between the bars.

★ **COACH'S CORNER**

Staying Safe

Whenever you work on any gymnastics apparatus, be sure to place floor **mats** (MATS) around the equipment. You should always work with a **spotter** (SPAHT er) nearby to help you and catch you if you fall.

When practicing on either the parallel bars or the horizontal bar, be sure to lower them to chest or head height. This way, you won't fall far if something goes wrong! Raise the bar gradually as you become more skilled.

The basic swing is the best way to start a routine on the horizontal bar.

SUPPORTS AND HANGS ON THE HORIZONTAL BAR

There are two basic types of movements on the horizontal bar. **Supports** (suh PAWRTS) hold your body up on your arms. **Hangs** (HANGZ) include all the swinging and hanging movements on the bar. Every competitive routine on the horizontal bar must include both supports and hangs. Some commonly performed supports and hangs are described in this chapter.

Front Support

1. Stand facing one side of the bar. Extend your arms and grab the bar in an overgrip.
2. Bend your knees and jump up. End with your arms supporting your weight and your hips resting against the bar. This is the front-support position.

Hip Pullover

1. Stand facing one side of the bar with your arms forward and your hands on the bar in an overgrip.
2. Jump forward, pulling your chest toward the bar. At the same time, **pike** (PIK) your body so that your legs swing under the bar.
3. Swing your legs over the top of the bar. Your body should follow.
4. Straighten your body as your legs come back down toward the floor. End in the front-support position.

Hip Circle Backward

To do a hip circle backward:
1. Start with a front-support mount.
2. Swing your legs forward slightly to gain momentum, then swing them backward.
3. At the top of the backswing, push yourself up until your legs, arms, and upper body are parallel to the floor.
4. Keep your legs together and let them move forward. When your hips strike the bar, pike your body and send your legs up to the far side. Pull with your arms, then circle around the bar and end in the front-support position.

This gymnast shows very good posture while practicing the hip pullover.

Hip circle forward

Hip Circle Forward

To do a hip circle forward:

1. Raise your chest and extend your body out as straight as you can as you leave the front-support position. Move forward until your body is parallel to the floor.

2. Pull against the bar with your hands and bend your head and chest underneath the bar. At the same time, pike your legs so that your hips are against the bar.

3. Circle the bar and end in the front-support position. As you circle, it's important to lead with your chest to build up enough momentum to complete the circle.

Single-Leg Swing-Up

For a single-leg swing-up:

1. Hang from the bar with your left leg tucked between your arms and hooked over the bar. Your right leg should be stretched out parallel to the floor.

2. Next, swing your right leg up to build momentum. Then swing it down, keeping it straight as you do so. At the same time, pull with your arms and swing upward. Your left leg should still be on the bar at the knee. Your right leg will be stretched out behind you. This is called the single-knee-support position.

★ **DID YOU KNOW?**

Gaining Momentum

To perform the single-leg circle, you'll need plenty of momentum. Be sure to keep your head and shoulders back at all times so they can lead the way over the bar. When you reach the top of the bar, pull hard with your arms to give yourself the final lift you need to complete the movement.

Single-Leg Circle Backward

To do a single-leg circle backward:

1. Start from the single-knee-support position.
2. Swing your right leg down. At the same time, push your body away from the bar and let yourself fall backward.
3. Circle beneath the bar, keeping your left knee hooked over the bar. End in the single-knee-support position.

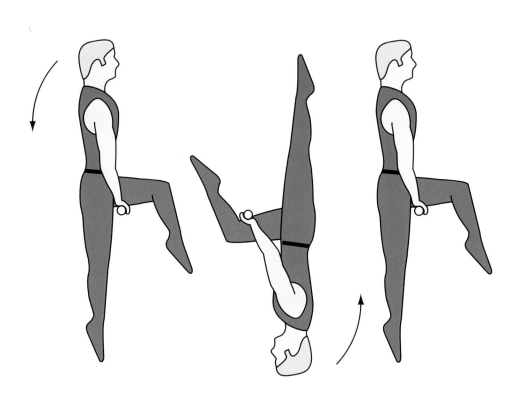

Single-leg circle backward

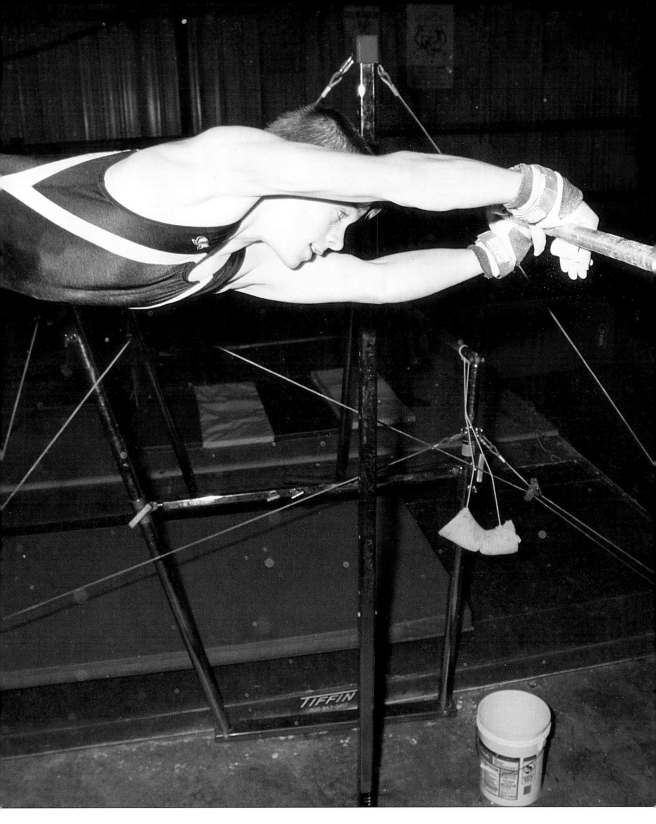

A gymnast practices his swing turn on the horizontal bar.

Single-leg Circle Forward

    For the single-leg circle forward:

1. Start from the single-knee-support position. But this time, hold the bar in a **reverse grip** (reh VERSS GRIP), with your thumb facing the front of the bar and your fingers curled around the back.

2. Push yourself up and forward. Let your head and chest lead the way as you circle the bar, then return to your original position.

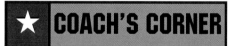

★ COACH'S CORNER

The Mixed Grip

    As you perform the swinging half turn left, the turning action will move the knuckles on your left hand beneath the bar. Meanwhile, the knuckles on your right hand will be above the bar and pointed in the direction of the swing. This is called a **mixed grip** (MIKST GRIP) because each hand is gripping the bar in a different way.

Free Swing

A free swing is the most important basic movement on the horizontal bar. You will use it again and again.

1. Hang straight from the bar with an overgrip.
2. Swing your legs up and forward, then back and down. Pump your legs on each forward swing to build momentum.
3. Don't let yourself swing too high, or you will lose your grip and fall!

Swinging Half Turn

To do a swinging half turn left:

1. Start with a free swing.
2. As you reach the top of your swing, turn your head and shoulders to the left.
3. Release your right hand, move it across your left hand, and grab the bar in an overgrip just beyond your left hand.
4. Complete the turn of your body so that you are facing front as you swing down. Be sure to keep your legs together.

5. To perform a swinging half turn right, simply move the left hand past your right hand, and turn to the right.

★ DID YOU KNOW?

The Giant Swing

Experienced gymnasts often perform a move called the giant swing. During this move, the gymnast swings all the way around the bar with his arms and legs completely straight. The pull on the gymnast's shoulders can be five times the force of gravity!

The Upstart

1. Swing forward with your body straight and stretched out. As you reach the top of the forward swing, lift your legs. Be sure to keep your arms straight.

2. When your ankles are level with the bar, swing your shoulders and body backward. At the same time, kick your feet toward the ceiling to gain momentum.

3. As you swing backward, hold the bar close to your thighs. Swing your body forward over the bar. Then swing your legs backward so that you end in the front-support position.

Swing to Back Support

Follow these directions to swing to the back-support position.

1. Swing forward strongly. As you reach the top of the forward swing, lift your legs until they are higher than the bar.

2. At the top of the forward swing, place your feet between your hands and under the bar. Your legs should be straight and parallel to the floor.

3. As you swing backward, stretch out your legs so that they reach over the bar.

4. Swing down into the back-support position, with your hands behind your hips and your weight on your arms. Your legs should be stretched over the front of the bar and pointed toward the floor.

★ COACH'S CORNER

Protecting Your Hands

Working on the bars is very hard on your hands. Constantly rubbing against the bars can cause blisters, scrapes, and cuts. To protect their hands, many gymnasts wear **hand guards** (HAND GAHRDZ) or grips until their hands toughen up and form calluses. You can also protect your hands by using gymnastics chalk, working in short sessions, and cupping the bar in your hands rather than gripping it tightly.

SWINGS, HOLDS, AND TUMBLES ON THE PARALLEL BARS

A routine on the parallel bars includes **swings** (SWINGZ), **holds** (HOLDZ), and **tumbling** (TUHM bling) moves. Balance is especially important when working on the bars. Your body should be straight, with your arms locked and your shoulders lined up over your hands.

Swings

Directions for performing some basic swings are listed in this section.

Forward Swing to Straddle-Seat Position

1. Start with the straight-arm support mount.
2. Swing both legs forward above the bars.
3. As soon as your legs clear the bars, open them and let them drop to either side, so you are sitting in a **straddle** (STRAD ul) seat on the bars. End with your back straight and your hands directly behind your legs.

Straddle-Seat Travel

1. Start from the straddle-seat position discussed above. Lean forward and grab the bars just in front of your thighs.
2. Swing your legs back and up, then down between the bars and high to the front. Separate your legs at the end of each forward swing.
3. End in the straddle-seat position. You can use this movement to travel forward all the way down the bars. To travel backward, just reverse the process.

Straight-arm Swing and Turn

For the more difficult straight-arm swing and turn:
1. Start from the straight-arm support position.
2. Lean to your right and pull your left hand off the bar.
3. Swing your body around and bring the front of your thighs against the right bar.
4. Move your left hand over to grab the right bar, and move your right hand over to the left bar.
5. As your hands move, turn your body to follow them. You will swing around to the right and end in the straight-arm support position, facing the opposite direction. To swing to the left, simply reverse the process.

A good basic move for a first time gymnast is the straddle-seat travel.

The swinging motion to gain momentum is important to many routines
on the parallel bars.

Swinging Dip Travel

A **dip** (DIP) is a basic arm position in which you support yourself on sharply bent arms. There are three elements to a successful dip. Your shoulders should be in front of your elbows. Your elbows should be bent at a 90-degree angle. And your forearms should be as straight as possible.

To do a swing dip travel:

1. Start with your arms straight. Swing your legs backward, then forward.

2. As your legs swing forward, lower yourself into a dip.

3. At the top of the forward swing, push your hands against the bar, straighten your arms, and push yourself forward. Your hands will leave the bars for an instant as you "hop" forward.

4. Continue to move down the bar by repeating step #3. To move backward, push away from the bar at the end of your backswing, instead of at the top of your forward swing.

The dip without travel is used as a conditioning element for girls and boys. Adding the travel is an advanced move you should work on with your coach's assistance.

Back Uprise

The back uprise is an advanced move that starts with an upper-arm support position. Begin with your arms straight and slowly drop down until you're resting on your upper arms. Your elbows should be bent sharply, and your hands should be in front of you, holding the bars.

1. Swing your legs back and forth to gain momentum.

2. Bring your legs into a pike position from a forward swing. Then swing them down hard and fast into a backswing.

3. As your legs swing back, pull hard on your arms and straighten them to push yourself away from the bars. Your body should be extended at an angle above the bars.

4. Swing down to end in a straight-arm support position.

Supporting your body with your upper arms as you gain momentum is an important part of the back uprise.

Holds

Only three hold positions are permitted during a competition routine on the parallel bars. Because hold positions require a combination of great balance and strength, they can often be the highlight of a bars routine.

Here is a basic hold position:

Shoulder Stand

1. Start from a straddle-seat position. Your hands should be just in front of your thighs.
2. Lean forward and lift your hips into the air. Your legs should clear the bar and leave you balancing on your bent arms for a moment.
3. As soon as you feel the weight on your arms, turn your bent elbows out. Let your upper arms drop to the bars and support your weight.
4. Continue raising your hips as your upper arms drop to the bars. Then bring your legs together.
5. Finish by raising your legs until they are straight. Your toes should be pointed at the ceiling and your back should be as straight as possible.

Putting your body in a pike position makes a backward roll easier.

Tumbling

Several tumbling moves that are performed during **floor exercises** (FLAWR EK ser SIZ ez) can also be performed on the parallel bars. Two of the simplest moves are forward and backward rolls.

Forward Roll

To do a forward roll:

1. Start in the straddle-seat position with your hands holding the bars in front of your thighs.
2. Lean forward, then place your upper arms on the bars and bend your elbows out to the side.
3. At the same time, move your hips up and forward until they pass over your head.
4. As soon as your hips are over your head, let go of the bars and move your hands forward to grab the bars just ahead of your back.
5. Continue the roll until you reach the end of the bars. Then return to the straddle-seat position.

Backward Roll

1. Start from the straddle-seat position. But this time, reach behind you to grab the bars.
2. Pike your body and roll along your back until your hips are over your head.
3. Let go of the bars and grab them again several inches in front of your head.
4. Continue rolling to the end of the bars and end in the straddle-seat position.

The Kip

A kip is a more difficult move.

1. With your hands in an overgrip, jump off the floor or springboard. Swing forward in the hollow position with legs in the pike position.

2. Extend forward and bring your feet toward your hands.

3. Raise your legs upward, then hop your hands to the top of the bar and support yourself on straight arms.

★ **COACH'S CORNER**

Changing the Ending

You don't have to end your forward or backward roll in the straddle-seat position. Instead keep your legs together and drop between the bars into the upper-arm support position.

DISMOUNTS

A good **dismount** (DISS MOUNT), or exit from the bars, adds a polished ending to your routine. Just as with dismounts in other gymnastics events, a dismount from the parallel bars or the horizontal bar should flow into a solid landing on the balls of your feet. Bend your knees to absorb the impact of landing. Do not take any extra steps or hops for balance. As soon as your feet touch the ground, drop your heels, straighten your body, and stand at attention.

Dismounts from the Parallel Bars

The simplest way to dismount the parallel bars is to swing forward on straight arms and lift your legs until they are parallel to the floor. Then push yourself up and away from the bars and straighten your legs so your feet are pointed toward the floor. Land on the balls of your feet, with your knees slightly bent.

Two more complicated dismounts are described as follows:

Rear Dismount

1. Start from a straight-arm support position. Pike your body and send your legs over the right bar.
2. As your legs clear the bar, push your left hand away from the left bar to drive your body sideways and over the right bar.
3. Straighten from the pike position as your legs start toward the floor.
4. Release the right bar with your right hand and let your left hand travel over to grab the right bar.
5. Drop to a landing outside the right bar with your left hand holding the bar and your right hand extended out.

Rear dismount

Practice landing in the same location after each routine.

Front Dismount

1. Start with a strong forward swing from the straight-arm support position.

2. Swing back until your body is extended above the bars, parallel to the floor. This position is called a **cast** (KAST).

3. At the top of your cast, push your left hand away from the left bar so it drives your body to the outside of the right bar.

4. Bring your left hand over to grab the right bar while you let go with the right hand and send that hand out to the side.

5. Finish by landing on both feet with your left hand holding the right bar. If you wish to land to the left of the bars, reverse the process.

Dismounts from the Horizontal Bar

You may have seen gymnasts perform amazing dismounts from the horizontal bar in competitions. You can learn dramatic dismounts as you become more experienced. Meanwhile, here are two simpler—but still exciting—dismounts to try.

Drop Swing Dismount

1. At the top of a backswing, let go of the bar and drop straight down to the floor.
2. Land on the balls of your feet with your arms stretched out for balance and your knees bent to absorb the impact. Then drop your heels and stand at attention.

Drop swing dismount

This gymnast shows the proper landing technique when performing a dismount.

Underswing Dismount

1. Start from the front-support position. Swing your legs forward and let your body follow them underneath the bar.

2. As you drop below the bar and straighten your arms, pike your body and swing your legs up to the far side of the bar. Then whip them forward. Stretch out your body as straight as you can.

3. Arch your back strongly and release the bar. Land on both feet with your arms raised above your head.

★ **DID YOU KNOW?**

Practice Each Element

The underswing dismount can be a little scary at first, so it's best to practice it in segments. At first, just drop back into a hang until you get used to the feel of this movement. Then add the pike. Then add the push forward with the body extended and release the bar. Practicing each element of the dismount separately will help you gain confidence and perform a more successful dismount when you're finally ready to attempt the complete move.

GLOSSARY

apparatus (AP uh RAT uhs) — a special piece of equipment for performing a gymnastic event

arch (AHRCH) — a position in which the upper and lower parts of your body form a slight curve

cast (KAST) — the most basic swing used by a gymnast on the uneven bars

dip (DIP) — a basic position in which you support yourself on sharply bent arms

dismount (DISS MOUNT) — to get off an apparatus

floor exercises (FLAWR EK ser SIZ ez) — a gymnastics event made up of a series of tumbling, dancing, and balancing moves performed on a cushioned floor

hand guards (HAND GAHRDZ) — soft leather "gloves" that fit over the middle two fingers and fasten around the wrist to protect the hands

hangs (HANGZ) — swinging and hanging movements on the horizontal bar

holds (HOLDZ) — moves in which a gymnast holds his body motionless

hollow (HAHL O) — a position where the body is stretched fully with a slightly rounded back

mat (MAT) — a padded surface that provides a soft, safe landing place for a gymnast

mixed grip (MIKST GRIP) — a two-handed grip in which each hand grips the bar a different way

GLOSSARY

mount (MOUNT) — to get on an apparatus

overgrip (O ver GRIP) — holding the bar with your fingers curled over the top

pike (PIK) — a position in which the legs are straight and the body is folded at the waist

pommel horse (PAHM ul HAWRS) — a gymnastics apparatus made up of a cushioned wooden "horse" with leather handles on the top

reverse grip (reh VERSS GRIP) — holding the bar with your thumbs pointing toward the front and your fingers curled around the back of the bar

routine (roo TEEN) — a combination of moves displaying a full range of skills

spotter (SPAHT er) — a coach or experienced gymnast who stands below a gymnast to give advice and catch him or her if she falls

straddle (STRAD ul) — a position in which the legs are held straight and apart across the apparatus

supports (suh PAWRTS) — positions in which a gymnast holds his body up on his arms

swings (SWINGZ) — movements back and forth from a hanging position

tumbling (TUHM bling) — gymnastics stunts such as rolling, somersaulting, and other acrobatic feats

FURTHER READING

Find out more about the parallel bars and the horizontal bar from these helpful books, magazines, and information sites:

- Feeney, Rik. *Gymnastics: A Guide for Parents and Athletes.* Indianapolis: Masters Press, 1992.
- Gutman, Dan. *Gymnastics.* New York: Viking, 1996.
- Marks, Marjorie. *A Basic Guide to Gymnastics: An Official U.S. Olympic Committee Sports Series.* Glendale, CA: Griffin Publishing, 1998.
- Peszek, Luan. *The Gymnastics Almanac.* Los Angeles: Lowell House, 1998.
- *USA Gymnastics Safety Handbook.* Indianapolis: USA Gymnastics, 1998.

- *USA Gymnastics*—This magazines covers American competitions and athletes, as well as major competitions leading up to the Olympics.
- *Technique*—This publication is geared toward coaches and judges.
- *International Gymnast*—This magazine covers both American and international competitions and athletes.

- www.usa-gymnastics.org
  This is the official Website of USA Gymnastics, the national governing body for gymnastics in the United States.
- www.ngja.org
  National Gymnastics Judges Association, Inc.
- www.ngja.org
  This is the official Website for the National Gymnastics Judges Association, Inc.

INDEX